EDGE BOOKS

PRO SPORTS
by the Numbers

PRO BASEBALL
by the Numbers

by Todd Kortemeier

Consultant:
Stew Thornley, MLB Official Scorer and Sports Historian/Author

CAPSTONE PRESS
a capstone imprint

Edge Books are published by Capstone Press, 1710 Roe Crest Drive, North Mankato, Minnesota 56003
www.mycapstone.com

Library of Congress Cataloging-in-Publication Data
Cataloging-in-publication information is on file with the Library of Congress.

ISBN 978-1-4914-9059-4 (library binding)
ISBN 978-1-4914-9063-1 (paperback)
ISBN 978-1-4914-9067-9 (ebook PDF)

Editorial Credits
Patrick Donnelly, editor
Nikki Farinella, designer and production specialist

Photo Credits
AP Images: 15, Carlos Osorio, cover (bottom), 1, Damon Tarver/Cal Sport Media, 21, Mark Alberti/Icon Sportswire, 10–11, Mark J. Terrill, cover (top), 20 (background); Chicago History Museum/Getty Images, 16; iStockphoto: gnagel, 6 (left), Juanmonino, 18 (bottom), Luevanos, 19 (top foreground); Newscom: Art Foxall/UPI, 17, Panworld Sports/Icon SMI, 5 (top); Red Line Editorial, 14; Shutterstock Images: aastock, 4, Alexey Pushkin, 23 (middle bottom), Antony McAulay, 6–7, AridOcean, 23 (top), B-A-C-O, 22–23 (top), chrupka, 12–13, Daniel M. Silva, 26–27, Eugene Buchko, 7 (top), Ffooter, 6 (right), Heath Oldham, 7 (bottom left), Jason KS Leung, 23 (middle top), karnizz, 18 (top), katatonia82, 4–5, 22, KoQ Creative, cover (top right), cover (bottom right), 5 (bottom), 7, 12, 20 (bottom), 23 (middle), 28, 29, Leonard Zhukovsky, 19 (top background), Mark Herreid, 7 (bottom right), Mike Flippo, 18 (middle), Nagel Photography, 24–25, Omer Yurdakul Gundogdu, 19 (bottom), phoelix, 23 (bottom), Steve Broer/Shutterstock Images, 8–9, Thumbelina, 22–23 (bottom), trialhuni, 28–29

Design Elements
Red Line Editorial (infographics), Shutterstock Images (perspective background, player silhouettes)

Printed in the United States of America in Mankato, Minnesota
102015   2015CAP

TABLE OF CONTENTS

> *"Baseball is a game between two teams of nine players each, under direction of a manager, played on an enclosed field in accordance with these rules, under jurisdiction of one or more **umpires**."*
> —Rule 1.01, Official Rules of Major League Baseball (MLB)

Numbers are a huge part of the game of baseball. Some are simple, as Rule 1.01 shows. Two teams. Nine players. One or more umpires. But beyond that, MLB history contains thousands of numbers that allow fans to measure and judge the feats of its great players. Read on to discover some of the most iconic numbers that our national pastime has to offer.

Timeline: Milestone Years of Baseball

1867
Candy Cummings throws the first curveball in a game.

1876
The National League (NL) begins play.

1901
The American League (AL) begins play.

1920
The office of commissioner of baseball is created.

1845
The first modern rules of baseball are developed.

1869
The Cincinnati Red Stockings are founded. This is the first professional team in baseball history.

1903
The first World Series takes place between AL champion Boston and NL champion Pittsburgh.

umpire: an official person who makes sure the game is played correctly and fairly
curveball: a type of pitch that spins away from a straight path as it approaches the batter

1947
Jackie Robinson breaks baseball's color barrier.

1994
A player strike cancels the last six weeks of the season and the World Series.

1961
MLB expands for the first time. The Los Angeles Angels and the new Washington Senators (replacing the team that became the Minnesota Twins) join the AL.

1997
Interleague play begins between the AL and the NL.

1975
The end of baseball's reserve clause starts the free agency era.

2012
MLB adds a second wild card spot to the postseason format.

1973
The AL adopts the designated hitter (DH) rule.

1995
The New York Yankees and Colorado Rockies are MLB's first wild card teams.

color barrier: an unwritten rule that kept African Americans from joining all-white sports teams
free agency: a system that allows players to jump from one team to another after their contracts are done
wild card: a team that makes the playoffs despite not having won its division

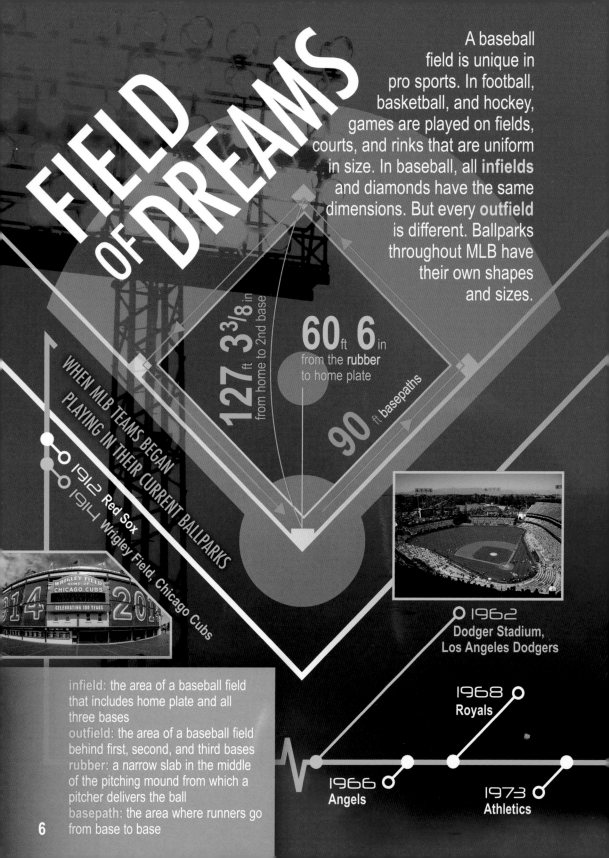

FIELD OF DREAMS

A baseball field is unique in pro sports. In football, basketball, and hockey, games are played on fields, courts, and rinks that are uniform in size. In baseball, all **infields** and diamonds have the same dimensions. But every **outfield** is different. Ballparks throughout MLB have their own shapes and sizes.

127 ft **3 ³/₈** in from home to 2nd base

60 ft **6** in from the **rubber** to home plate

90 ft basepaths

WHEN MLB TEAMS BEGAN PLAYING IN THEIR CURRENT BALLPARKS

1912 Red Sox

1914 Wrigley Field, Chicago Cubs

1962
Dodger Stadium,
Los Angeles Dodgers

1968
Royals

1966
Angels

1973
Athletics

infield: the area of a baseball field that includes home plate and all three bases

outfield: the area of a baseball field behind first, second, and third bases

rubber: a narrow slab in the middle of the pitching mound from which a pitcher delivers the ball

basepath: the area where runners go from base to base

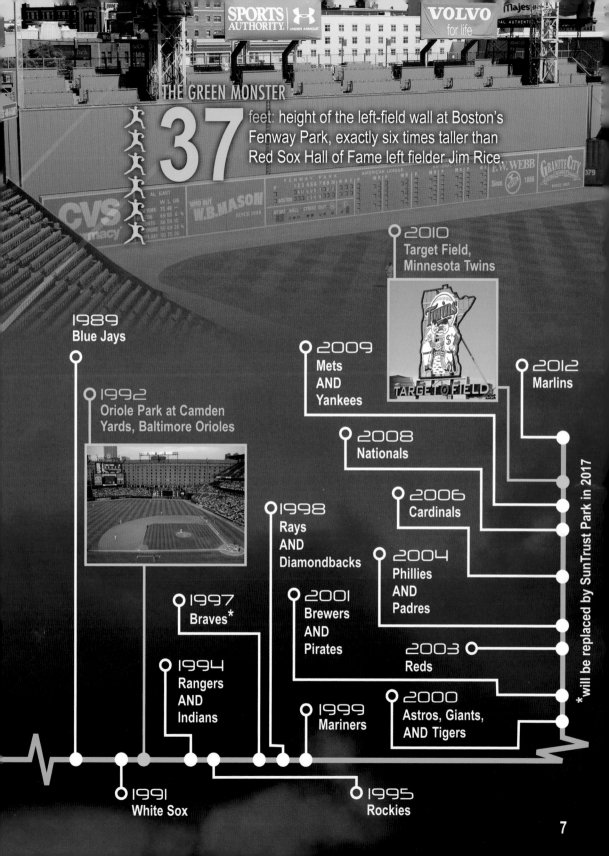

THE GREEN MONSTER

37

feet: height of the left-field wall at Boston's Fenway Park, exactly six times taller than Red Sox Hall of Fame left fielder Jim Rice.

2010
Target Field,
Minnesota Twins

1989
Blue Jays

2009
Mets
AND
Yankees

2012
Marlins

1992
Oriole Park at Camden
Yards, Baltimore Orioles

2008
Nationals

2006
Cardinals

1998
Rays
AND
Diamondbacks

2004
Phillies
AND
Padres

1997
Braves*

2001
Brewers
AND
Pirates

2003
Reds

1994
Rangers
AND
Indians

1999
Mariners

2000
Astros, Giants,
AND Tigers

*will be replaced by SunTrust Park in 2017

1991
White Sox

1995
Rockies

THE HOME RUN RECORD

The home run is one of the most exciting plays in baseball. Some of the game's greatest players were masters of the long ball. Babe Ruth, Willie Mays, and Hank Aaron are some of the names that come to mind. But home run records have not been without controversy.

MLB Record Watch: Most Home Runs in a Season

Years the Home Run Record Lasted	1876–1878	1879–1882	1883	1884–1918	1919	1920	1921–1926
Home runs	5	9	14	27	29	54	59

THE EFFECT OF PERFORMANCE-ENHANCING DRUGS

2007

The Mitchell Report was released in 2007. It named 89 players who were linked to performance-enhancing drugs (PEDs). Some of these players were all-time greats, such as Barry Bonds. He holds the MLB single-season and career home run records. New rules and procedures for PED testing were established in 2005. Since that time the home run totals have returned to more normal levels.

60

61

70

73

1996

Eddie Murray became the 15th player to hit 500 career home runs. Ten more players joined the club between 1998 and 2009. No other stretch of years saw nearly as many new members.

1961–1994

Five players hit 50 home runs in a season. From 1995 through 2014, it happened 25 times.

1998

Before 1998 only two players had ever hit 60 home runs in a season. That number doubled in 1998. From 1998 through 2001, three players combined for six 60-homer seasons.

1927–1960

1961–1997

1998–2000

2001–present

TOOLS OF THE TRADE

Baseball can appear to be a simple game. The action starts with a bat hitting the ball. But a lot goes into these two pieces of equipment.

BAT

RULE 3.02

defines a bat as a "smooth, round stick."

42 INCHES
maximum length of a bat

40,000

approximate number of trees used to make one season's worth of Louisville Slugger bats

Weight range in ounces of bats used in MLB history

30 ——●——————————●—————— 48

32
Miguel Cabrera's bat

42
Babe Ruth's bat

MLB PLAYERS WHO USE LOUISVILLE SLUGGER BATS

60%

APPROXIMATE TIME NEEDED TO MAKE ONE BAT

50 SECONDS

TYPES OF WOOD USED TO MAKE BATS

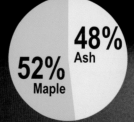

48% Ash

52% Maple

$900,000

number of balls Rawlings supplies to MLB every season

72 DOLLARS
cost of 12 MLB baseballs

5.5 MILLION DOLLARS
amount that each team spends on baseballs every year

108
number of stitches in a baseball

RULE 3.01

defines a ball as a "sphere formed by yarn wound around a small core of cork." All official MLB baseballs are made by Rawlings.

9–9.25 INCHES
circumference of a baseball

2.75 INCHES
maximum diameter

1 INCH
maximum depth of the "cup" at the end of the barrel

circumference: the distance around something
diameter: a straight line through the center of a circle, from one side to another

A GLOBAL GAME, STILL AMERICA'S

MLB teams have 40 players on their expanded **rosters**. That is, each team can have up to 40 players signed to major league contracts. For most of the season, only 25 of them can be on the major league roster at one time. If all major league players in 2014 were condensed into one 40-man roster, here is where the players would be from.

Canada
17

United States
988
PLAYERS

Dominican Republic
146

Mexico
11

Bahamas
1

Puerto Rico
23

Cuba
26

Nicaragua
4

Aruba
1

Jamaica
1

Curacao
5

Panama
5

Colombia
6

Venezuela
102

Brazil
2

United States 71.25%	
Canada 1.25%	
Caribbean 22.5%	
South America 2.5%	
East Asia 1.875%	
Other 0.625%	

roster: a list of names, often members of a team

PASTIME

Baseball was invented in the United States, but it is gaining popularity around the globe. Players from all over the world are MLB stars. But the United States still leads the pack.

Netherlands
1

Germany
3

South Korea
2

Japan
12

Taiwan
4

Saudi Arabia
1

Australia
3

N
W E
S

BASEBALL
BY THE 3s

GREAT PLAYERS TO WEAR

BABE RUTH

3

ALEX RODRIGUEZ

3

JIMMIE FOXX

3

HARMON KILLEBREW

3

HAROLD BAINES

3

The number three comes up often in baseball. From great players to important statistics, this number links many aspects of the game.

1933
THE FIRST MLB ALL-STAR GAME

3
STRIKES YOU'RE OUT!

	1	2	3	4	5	6	7	8	9	R	H	E
VISITOR	0	1	2							3	4	1
HOME	0	0	3							3	5	0

BALLS
0

STRIKES
3
per batter

OUTS
3
in an inning

3 numbered bases

3 home runs for Albert Pujols of the St. Louis Cardinals in Game 3 of the 2011 World Series

2

1

3

LEFT, CENTER, RIGHT
OUTFIELDERS
The Alou brothers were the only all-brother outfield in MLB history. They played for the San Francisco Giants in 1963.

CY vs. "CY"

CY YOUNG VS. CY YOUNG AWARD WINNER

CY YOUNG

COMPLETE GAMES	48
WINS	36
LOSSES	12
STARTS	49
SHUTOUTS	9
INNINGS	453
STRIKEOUTS	168

Quality starting pitching has always been important in baseball. But the way starters are used has changed dramatically. **Complete games** and **shutouts** used to be fairly common. These days, starters rarely go the distance. To better understand this point, take a look at the 1892 statistics for Cy Young. MLB's top pitching award is named for him. See how his numbers compare with the 2014 performance of Clayton Kershaw. He won the NL Cy Young Award that year.

CLAYTON
KERSHAW

COMPLETE GAMES **6**

WINS **21**

LOSSES **3**

STARTS **27**

SHUTOUTS **2**

INNINGS **198 1/3**

STRIKEOUTS **239**

complete game: when the starting pitcher throws every inning for his team in a game
shutout: when an opposing team does not score

17

TAKE ME OUT
TO THE BALLGAME

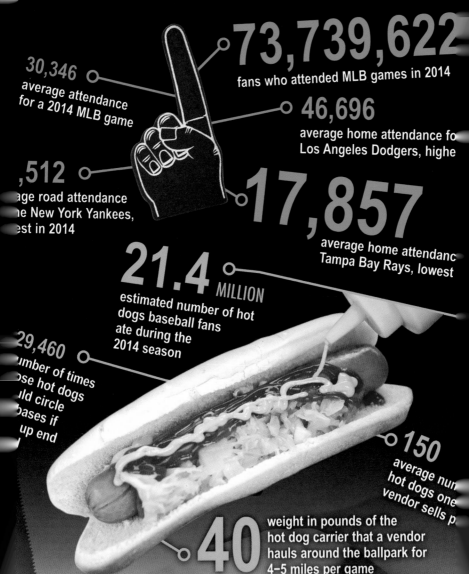

73,739,622
fans who attended MLB games in 2014

30,346
average attendance for a 2014 MLB game

46,696
average home attendance fo
Los Angeles Dodgers, highe

17,857
average home attendanc
Tampa Bay Rays, lowest

,512
age road attendance
he New York Yankees,
est in 2014

21.4 MILLION
estimated number of hot dogs baseball fans ate during the 2014 season

29,460
umber of times
ose hot dogs
ld circle
ases if
up end

150
average num
hot dogs one
vendor sells p

40
weight in pounds of the hot dog carrier that a vendor hauls around the ballpark for 4–5 miles per game

$16.37
cheapest average ticket
in MLB, San Diego Padres

$27.93
average price of an MLB game ticket

$52.32
most expensive
average ticket in MLB,
Boston Red Sox

$200.31
average cost for a family of four to attend
an MLB game: four tickets, four sodas, four
hot dogs, parking, two programs, and two
souvenir caps

12.1 MILLION
number of viewers for the 2014 All-Star Game

23.5 MILLION
number of viewers who
tuned in to Game 7 of the
2014 World Series

95,000
average number of households in
St. Louis that tuned in to watch
Cardinals games in 2014, the most
in baseball

DUALPERSPECTIVES

Toeing the Rubber

105
fastest pitch ever recorded, by Aroldis Chapman

97 average speed of Yordano Ventura's fastball

90 speed of an average fastball

81.7 average speed of A. J. Burnett's curveball

76 average speed of R. A. Dickey's knuckleball

62.1 slowest average speed for any 2014 pitch

CONTACT RATE FOR ALL MLB HITTERS IN 2014

65%	62%	64%	66%	69%
81%	81%	84%	83%	79%
84%	91%	91%	88%	74%
69%	85%	86%	79%	52%
31%	52%	54%	41%	17%

Every hitter's strike zone is different. The nine squares in the center of the chart are spots in the strike zone. The squares on the chart's edges would usually be called balls.

60 ft **6** in from mound to home plate

110 mph
speed a 90 mph fastball can come back at the pitcher if it is hit squarely

.251
overall MLB batting average in 2014

4,145 lbs
amount of force from
an average swing

150 milliseconds needed
to swing the bat

250
brain signals the body
to start the swing

100
see the ball

225
decide whether and
where to swing

MILLISECONDS

175
determine speed,
spin, and location
of the ball

400
MILLISECONDS
TOTAL TIME FOR
A 90 MPH
FASTBALL TO
REACH THE
PLATE

The mound is
10 INCHES high,
allowing a downward
angle that makes a
pitch tougher to hit.

The batter's box is **4** feet wide

and **6** feet long.

THE LONG BALL

Mike Trout hit the longest home run of the 2014 MLB season. It traveled 489 feet into the fountain at Kauffman Stadium in Kansas City. That's farther than:

363 FEET
SATURN V ROCKET

489 FEET

11.75
78-PASSENGER SCHOOL BUSES

24.45
GIRAFFES

360 FEET
FOOTBALL FIELD

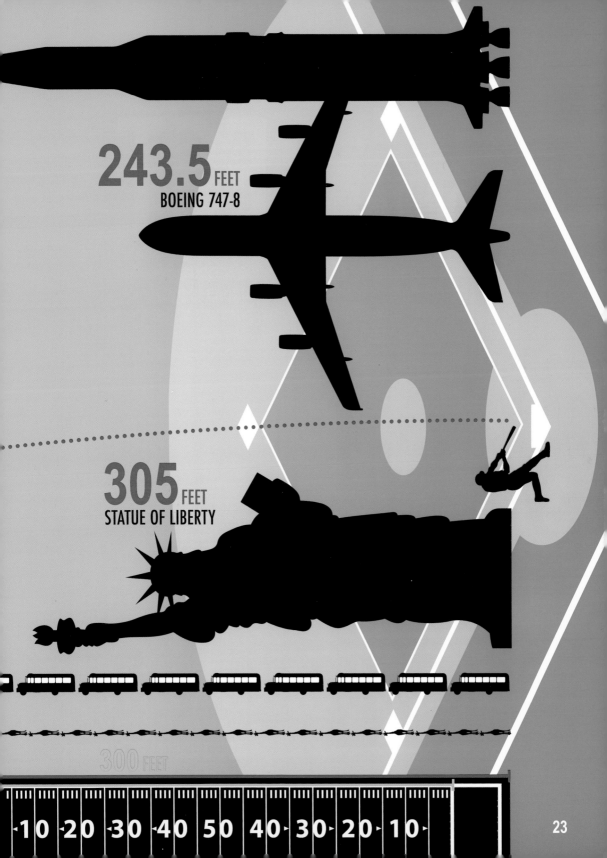

243.5 FEET
BOEING 747-8

305 FEET
STATUE OF LIBERTY

300 FEET

10 20 30 40 50 40 30 20 10

THE BEST OF THE BEST

Babe Ruth. Ty Cobb. Willie Mays. Sandy Koufax. These all-time greats live on forever in the National Baseball Hall of Fame. From the **Negro Leagues** to the major leagues, it takes some pretty big numbers to get there.

310 members of the Baseball Hall of Fame

- MLB PLAYERS
- NEGRO LEAGUE PLAYERS
- EXECUTIVES
- MANAGERS
- UMPIRES

Negro Leagues: collective name for leagues of exclusively African-American players, active during a time in which they were not allowed to play Major League Baseball

Numbers

There are no statistical criteria to get into the Hall of Fame. But there are some milestones that many in the Hall share.

500 HOME RUN CLUB

16 OF **21**
eligible members are in the Hall of Fame

3,000 HIT CLUB

25 OF **26**
eligible members are in the Hall of Fame

300 WINS CLUB

23 OF **24**
eligible members are in the Hall of Fame

3,000 STRIKEOUT CLUB

14 OF **16**
eligible members are in the Hall of Fame

Hall of Fame Eligibility

10 SEASONS
minimum length of a player's MLB career to be eligible

75 %
amount of the vote a player needs to be elected

5 YEARS
time a player must be retired before going on the ballot

15 YEARS
maximum time a player can be on the ballot

RETIRED NUMBERS

A uniform number can be strongly associated with the player who wears it. No. 7: Mickey Mantle. No. 9: Ted Williams. These numbers become synonymous with the players. Some teams choose to honor those great players by never giving their number to another player. This is called retiring a number.

Players and Managers with Numbers Retired by More than One Team

HANK AARON
(44) (44)

SPARKY ANDERSON
(10) (11)

ROD CAREW
(29) (29)

ROLLIE FINGERS
(34) (34)

CARLTON FISK
(27) (72)

REGGIE JACKSON
(9) (44)

GREG MADDUX
(31) (31)

FRANK ROBINSON
(20) (20)

NOLAN RYAN
(30) (34) (34)

CASEY STENGEL
(37) (37)

Retired Numbers per Team

BABE RUTH

LOU GEHRIG

	50	43	44	51	36
	30	30	34	34	35	32
	41	20	10	29	27	19	31	20
	51	34	37	10	10	26	24	4	19	14
12	12	17	20	26	14	5	8	11	9	1	6	1

Mariners · Marlins · Blue Jays · Rays · Rockies · Diamondbacks · Rangers · Mets · Royals · Nationals · Angels · Athletics · Brewers · Padres · Phillies

42

Jackie Robinson was the first player to break the color barrier. His team, the Dodgers, retired his number. Then in 1997 MLB retired No. 42 throughout the league to honor Robinson too. No. 42 is also retired by the Cardinals for Bruce Sutter and by the Yankees for Mariano Rivera, two players whose careers began before 1997.

EXCLUSIVE CLUBS

Baseball teams are sometimes called clubs. But the word has other meanings in the sport as well. Some statistical landmarks are considered signs of true greatness. These clubs contain the best of the best.

40-40 CLUB

	YR	HR	SB
Jose Canseco	1988	42	40
Barry Bonds	1996	42	40
Alex Rodriguez	1998	42	46
Alfonso Soriano	2006	46	41

40 home runs (HR) and 40 stolen bases (SB) in a season

20-20-20-20 CLUB

	YR	2B	3B	HR	SB
Frank "Wildfire" Schulte	1911	30	21	21	23
Willie Mays	1957	26	20	35	38
Curtis Granderson	2007	38	23	23	26
Jimmy Rollins	2007	38	20	30	41

20 doubles (2B), 20 triples (3B), 20 home runs (HR), and 20 stolen bases (SB) in a season

UNBREAKABLE

Some numbers may never be matched. These are some of the most unbreakable records in baseball.

2,632 Cal Ripken Jr.'s consecutive games played streak. At the end of the 2014 season, the longest active streak belonged to Atlanta's Freddie Freeman, with 168.

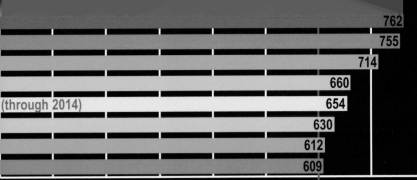

Player	Home Runs
Barry Bonds	762
Hank Aaron	755
Babe Ruth	714
Willie Mays	660
Alex Rodriguez (through 2014)	654
Ken Griffey Jr.	630
Jim Thome	612
Sammy Sosa	609

100 200 300 400 500 600 700

600 CLUB
600 home runs in a career

3,000 CLUB
3,000 hits in a career

29 PLAYERS

56 Joe DiMaggio's hitting streak. Pete Rose's 44-game streak in 1978 is the next closest since 1900.

59 Wins in a season by Charles "Old Hoss" Radbourn in 1884. Since 1935, only one pitcher has won even 30 games in a season—Denny McLain, who won 31 for the Detroit Tigers in 1968.

75 Complete games pitched in a season by Will White in 1879. James Shields's 11 complete games in 2011 are the most in this century.

1,406 Career stolen bases for Rickey Henderson. Henderson smashed Lou Brock's record of 938, and that remains the second-highest total.

Glossary

basepath (BAYSS-path)—the area where runners go from base to base

circumference (sur-KUHM-fur-uhnss)—the distance around something

color barrier (KUH-luhr BAYR-ee-uhr)—an unwritten rule that kept African Americans from joining all-white sports teams

complete game (kuhm-PLEET GAME)—when the starting pitcher throws every inning for his team in a game

curveball (KURV-bawl)—a type of pitch that spins away from a straight path as it approaches the batter

diameter (dye-AM-uh-tur)—a straight line through the center of a circle, from one side to another

free agency (FREE AY-juhn-see)—a system that allows players to jump from one team to another after their contracts are done

infield (IN-feeld)—the area of a baseball field that includes home plate and all three bases

Negro Leagues (NEE-groh LEEGZ)—collective name for leagues of exclusively African-American players, active during a time in which they were not allowed to play Major League Baseball

outfield (OUT-feeld)—the area of a baseball field behind first, second, and third bases

roster (ROS-tur)—a list of names, often members of a team

rubber (RUHB-ur)—a narrow slab in the middle of the pitching mound from which a pitcher delivers the ball

shutout (SHUHT-out)—when an opposing team does not score

umpire (UHM-pire)—an official person who makes sure the game is played correctly and fairly

wild card (WILDE KARD)—a team that makes the playoffs despite not having won its division

Read More

Adamson, Thomas K. *Baseball: The Math of the Game*. Sports Math. Mankato, Minn.: Capstone Press, 2012.

Jacobs, Greg. *The Everything Kids' Baseball Book: From Baseball's History to Today's Favorite Players—With Lots of Home Run Fun in Between*. Avon, Mass.: Adams Media, 2014.

Critical Thinking Using the Common Core

1. Many great players have been left out of the Hall of Fame because they have been suspected of using performance-enhancing drugs. Do you think that is fair? Why or why not? (Key Ideas and Details)

2. Many MLB players come from countries outside the United States. Why do you think baseball is especially popular in those areas? Do you think this trend will continue? (Integration of Knowledge and Ideas)

Internet Sites

FactHound offers a safe, fun way to find Internet sites related to this book. All of the sites on FactHound have been researched by our staff.

Visit *www.facthound.com*

Type in this code: 9781491490594

Check out projects, games and lots more at
www.capstonekids.com

Index